Welding Made Simple: The Ultimate Beginner's Handbook

Christopher .K Alston

All rights reserved. Copyright © 2023 Christopher .K Alston

Funny helpful tips:

Practice mutual admiration; it boosts self-esteem and connection.

Limit processed meats; they can be high in sodium and preservatives.

Welding Made Simple: The Ultimate Beginner's Handbook : Master the Art of Welding with this Comprehensive Guide for Beginners.

Life advices:

Your legacy is woven through the lives you touch; make every interaction count.

Stay open-minded; flexibility in thought broadens horizons.

Introduction

The guide on welding for beginners is a comprehensive resource that introduces newcomers to the world of welding. It covers various welding techniques and their practical applications, making it easier for beginners to understand the diversity of welding processes. Additionally, the guide explains the essential welding machines and tools required for successful welding projects, offering insights into the equipment used in welding workshops.

Setting up a proper welding workshop is crucial for beginners, and this guide provides guidance on selecting suitable locations, welding tables, and welding machines. Safety is a top priority in welding, and the guide emphasizes the importance of welding safety, including protective gear and preventive measures to ensure a secure working environment.

Novice welders can benefit from the valuable welding tips and techniques presented in the guide. These tips help beginners improve their welding skills, produce high-quality welds, and avoid common mistakes. Moreover, the guide provides guidance on evaluating the quality of welds, enabling beginners to assess their work accurately.

For practical experience, the guide offers welding projects that beginners can undertake. These projects serve as hands-on learning opportunities and allow newcomers to apply their newly acquired welding knowledge and skills. Additionally, the guide covers the concept of welding repair, providing essential information on initiating weld repairs and handling post-repair operations.

Overall, this guide serves as a valuable resource for individuals entering the world of welding, offering guidance, safety measures, practical projects, and tips to help beginners become proficient in welding techniques.

Contents

Chapter 1: Welding, Techniques, and Applications. 1
    Types of welding and their applications 1
Chapter 2: Welding Machines And Tools 4
Chapter 3: How To Set Up Your Welding Workshop 20
    How to Choose A Welding Location 20
    How To Choose A Welding Table 22
    How To Choose Your Welding Machine 22
Chapter 4: Welding Safety 25
Chapter 5: Welding Tips for Beginners 31
Chapter 6: How to Know If You Are Welding Correctly 35
Chapter 7: Welding Projects 38
    Outdoor Fireplace 39
    Wine Bottle Holder 42
    Barbecue Pit 44
    Welded Portraits Project 47
    Corner Desks 49
    Firewood Storage Dolly 51
    Hanging Shelves 53
    Steel Flower Welding Project 55
    Height Adjusting Stools 57
    Star Decor 59
    Welding Trolley Project 61
    Hanging Steel Pan Rack 64
    Simple Pencil Holder 67

- Welding Table 69
- Campfire Grill 72
- Suspension Stool 75
- Simple Garden bench 77
- Modern Outdoor Table 80
- TIG-Welded Fruit Bowl 83
- Metal Storage Rack 85

Chapter 8: Welding Repair 87
- What Is Repair Welding? 87
- Getting Started On Weld Repairs 88
- Post-Repair Operation 91

Chapter 1: Welding, Techniques, and Applications.

What is welding?

Welding is the process of heating pieces of metal using a flame or electricity to a melting point so that they fuse. We call the fused metal joint a weldment.

Types of welding and their applications

There are many types of welding, including MIG welding, TIG welding, ARC welding, gas welding, and flux-cored arc welding.

Metal Inert Gas (MIG) Welding

This is the easiest type of welding for beginners to learn. This type of welding uses an electric arc to melt two materials together to form a joint. However, a continuous solid wire electrode is used. It is heated and filled from a welding gun into the weld pool. MIG welding is ideal for dissimilar metals such as carbon steel/aluminum and carbon steel/ copper.

Applications of MIG welding include:

- Most types of sheet metal welding such as iron welding, copper welding, stainless steel welding, and aluminum welding
- The automotive industry, for example, welding component engine parts, fuel injectors, fuel filters, air and conditioning equipment, and transmission parts
- Home improvement industry such as replacing damaged pipes, cooking appliances, kitchen cabinets, countertops, and window seals
- Fabrication of pressure vessels and steel structures

Tungsten Inert Gas Welding (TIG)

This process uses a tungsten electrode to create an arc between the metals and is ideal for fusing hard metals like steel, copper, cobalt, and aluminum.

Applications of TIG welding include:

- Automotive industry
- Aerospace industry
- Auto body repairs
- Home appliances such as door handles
- Bike frames and lawnmowers

Flux-cored arc welding

This welding process uses heat produced by an electric arc to fuse the welt joint of the base metal. There are two types of flux-cored arc welding: self-shielded flux-cored welding, which solely relies on the flux core for shielding the weld pool, and gas-shielded flux-cored welding, which uses a shielding gas to protect the weld area.

Applications of flux-cored arc welding include:

- Shipbuilding
- Railroads
- Industrial piping
- Manufacturing plants
- Maintenance and repair

Gas tungsten arc welding

This process uses a tungsten electrode to make a weld. The heat from a concentrated flame melts metals and then joins them. The electrode rod adds the filler metal to the metal base, and shielding gas helps protect the pool arc from the atmosphere or contamination. This type of welding is ideal for welding light metals such as magnesium, aluminum, and copper.

Applications of Gas tungsten arc welding include:

- Joining thin metals such as copper, aluminum, and magnesium.
- Automobile and aircraft industries.
- Fabrication of sheet metal.

What is shielding gas, and what role does it play?

The shielding gas protects the solidifying molten weld from moisture, impurities in the air, and oxygenation, which may lessen the durability of the weld and its ability to tolerate corrosion by changing the features of the welded joint. It also plays the role of cooling down the welding gun.

Shielding gas is classifiable as inert or inactive. When using the MIG welding method, you use inert shielding gases which do not react with the molten weld. Examples of inert shielding gases include argon and helium. When using the gas welding method, inactive shielding gases are your option. Examples of active shielding gases include carbon dioxide and oxygen.

Before you can even begin welding, you must be aware of the tools you need. Let us look at that in the following chapter:

Chapter 2: Welding Machines And Tools

Before you start welding, it is also vital to know the different types of welding machines and learn their uses.

MIG machine

A MIG welding machine includes a welding gun, an electrode spool, an electrode feeder, a power supply, and shielding gas. You do not need a gas tank because the MIG machine doesn't use an external shielding gas.

The MIG machine does not weld on rusty or painted material, which is why it's important to clean up the materials first. It is also the easiest machine to use. The materials recommended for use with the MIG machine include

- Steel
- Aluminum
- Magnesium

- Carbon steel
- Nickel
- Silicon bronze

Stick welding machine

A stick welding machine has the welding leads, ground clamp, electrode holder, and the machine itself. This machine uses flux-covered electrode sticks of different sizes. The flux is important because it protects the stick welding machine from contamination. Also, the machine does not use an external shielding gas, meaning there is no need for a gas tank. The materials recommended for use with stick welding machine include

- Stainless steel
- Cast iron
- Steel

Flux-cored arc welding machine

This has a continuously-fed flux-filled electrode, so there is no need to stop and restart. Also, it produces fewer fumes and wastes fewer electrodes. When making welds using the flux-cored arc welding machine, you do not need an external shielding gas; therefore, a gas tank is unnecessary. The materials recommended for use with flux-cored arc welding include

- Carbon steels
- Cast iron
- Stainless steel [some]
- Nickle-based alloy

TIG welding machine

This machine is complicated and requires both hands: one hand holds the welding torch while the other feeds the filler. You also need to use a remote or a foot pedal to increase or lower the amps needed when welding.

The good thing is that although complicated at first, you can use this machine on a wide range of metal thicknesses. This machine uses an external shielding gas, making a gas tank necessary. The materials recommended for use with the TIG welding machine include

- Copper
- Steel
- Brass
- Stainless steel
- Aluminum
- Magnesium

- Titanium

Plasma arc welding machine

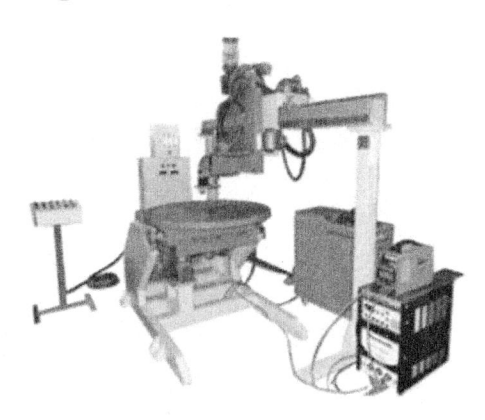

This large industrial-sized machine mostly used in aircraft manufacturing has an anode surrounding the electrode, which acts as a shield for the electrode. The anode protects the electrode from the powdery filler used for the plasma arc welding process.

Energy beam welding machine

This is a welding machine for industrial use only. You cannot use it at home since you must carry out welding in a vacuum to prevent the atmospheric absorption of the electron beam. The advantage of using this machine is that it can weld thick and thin metals.

Industries that use the energy beam welding machine include automotive, military, medical, oil and gas, power generation, and aerospace.

Atomic hydrogen welding machine

As a beginner welder, you will need to gain some experience before operating the atomic hydrogen welding machine since using it is not beginner-friendly.

For the welding process, an electric arc forms between two tungsten electrodes. The filler metal is usually added separately for this type of welding process. Only hydrogen is used as the shielding gas.

A benefit of using this machine is that it applies to both thick and thin metals. A disadvantage is that it is very costly. The materials usable with the atomic hydrogen welding machine include:

- Stainless steel
- Ferrous and non-ferrous metals

- Some special alloys

Submerged arc welding machine

This is an automated or semi-automated portable machine. You do not require much experience to operate it. An arc forms between the base metal and a continuously fed electrode during the welding process, producing a high-quality weld.

You do not use a shielding gas. Instead, you use a reusable powdered flux, thereby reducing waste. Materials recommended for use with the submerged arc welding include:

- Stainless steel
- Steel
- Nickel alloys
- Steel alloys

Gas welding oxy acetylene machine

This machine works better with thinner materials in contrast to thicker ones. You use fuel gas and oxygen to weld, which acts as a heating medium. The flame produced at the end of the torch melts the metal base and filler to form a weld. A benefit of using this machine is that it is portable. The materials recommended for use with the machine are iron-based or ferrous.

Essential Welding Tools

Let us also look at some tools you need to have before you can begin welding.

Welding Gloves

These are essential to any welding because they help protect your hands from extreme heat, electrical shock, and radiation and provide a good grip as they are made of robust fabrics and insulation. You can find them in any store that sells gloves, but when purchasing them, understand that there are two types.

> 1. **TIG welding gloves** are thin and soft, with a tighter fit to allow movement while holding the torch and rod.

2. **MIG welding gloves** are thick, with padding on the back of the hand.

Auto-Darkening Welding Helmet

A welding helmet is important because it protects your face from the flames and sparks that could damage your eyes and skin. An auto-darkening welding helmet has features such as multiple arc sensors and an auto-darkening filter lens that protects your eyes from the lights emitted from the heated metal and welding tools.

Welding pliers

You will need welding pliers for the following purposes:

- Loosening and tightening the contact tip as it gets worn out.
- Removing nozzles from the MIG gun.
- Removing welder spatter with the tips of the pliers.
- Wire drawing.
- Wire cutting.

Welding Magnets

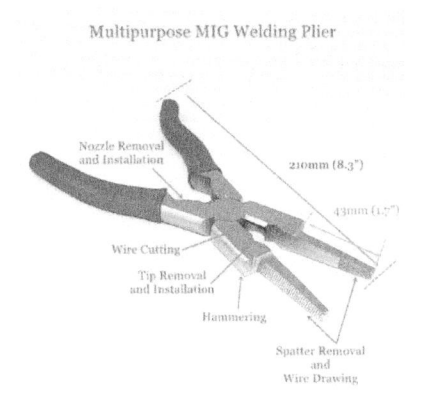

Welding magnets help hold metal parts in position as you manipulate and weld them with ease. They can stick to any metal and hold them at 45, 90, and 135-degrees angles and work better than clamps since they are more accurate.

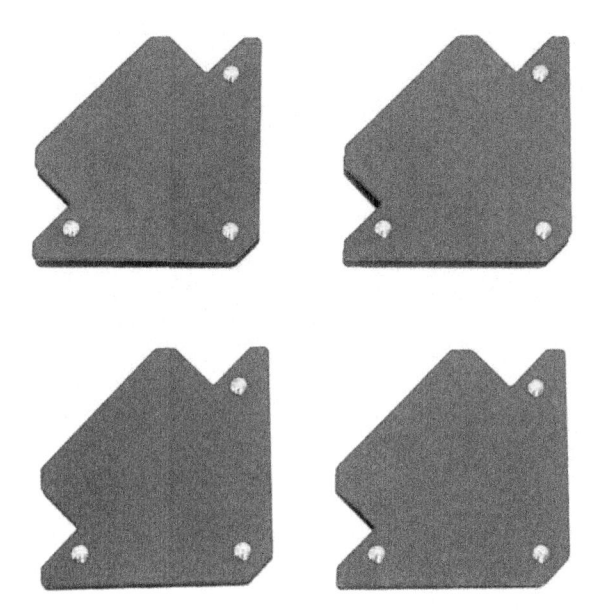

Angle Grinder

Angle grinders are used to cut metal, grind grooves, smoothen welds, and remove rust. It effectively cleans up the slag left over after welding.

Speed Square

This angular measuring device is shaped like a right triangle and is used to mark angles, common lines, and make square cuts on boards.

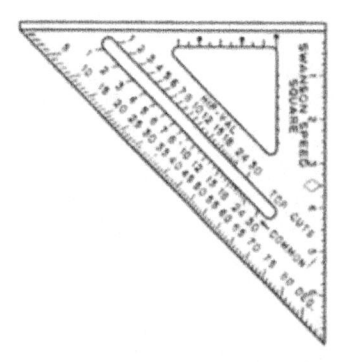

Chipping Hammer

This tool helps remove welding slag and spatter from along the sides of the weld as the metal melts into the weldment.

Sheet Metal Gauge

It is useful in measuring the thickness of your working metal. The material thickness decreases with an increase in the gauge number and increases with a decrease in the gauge number.

Metal File

The metal file helps remove burrs and rough edges from the cut metal. It cuts metal pieces using teeth.

Welding Boots

Welding boots have steel-reinforced toes and stout leather to protect your feet from the hot molten metal that falls while you are working. They also protect your feet from injury by heavy welding equipment.

Welding Sleeves

These are detachable sleeves made from either non-flammable fabric or leather with suspenders to hold them in place. They are important because they protect your skin and clothes from damage as the metal sparks fly around.

Welding Goggles

Sometimes wearing a helmet is a bit cumbersome. You may want something simple you can put on and take off with ease. Welding goggles are comfortable and lightweight. Although the protection they provide is limited, they protect your eyes from the sparks produced when welding.

C clamp

It is shaped like the letter c hence the name c clamp. It's main use is holding pieces of metal in place when welding them.

Chapter 3: How To Set Up Your Welding Workshop

This chapter will walk you through setting up your workshop for welding, starting from location to equipment.

How to Choose A Welding Location

As a beginner, you do not need to have a big space for your welding work. However, you do need to decide how much space you will need. Although a big space is not mandatory, you need enough space.

The items you plan to work with are an important consideration when planning your workspace. Bear in mind that the space ought to be big enough to allow you to move items around without colliding with other equipment, tools, or projects.

You also need to have plenty of room for your welding equipment. You certainly do not want a disorganized and cramped up workshop! The equipment may not take much space at first, but when you start your welding project, it will become apparent that the supplies you need take up more space.

Lastly, keep away any flammable material from your workshop. Sparks can fly quite a distance when making some welds, and fire is the last thing we want in a workshop.

Having considered your workshop space, you can set it up, whether it's simple or not, as long as it meets the following requirements:

- **Proper ventilation**: Welding may expose you to dangerous gases produced, for example, when you use electrodes with special coatings. Inhaling these gases is hazardous for your health. To stay healthy, you must ensure your welding space has proper ventilation before starting any welding work. If you have windows or doors in your welding workshop, you can open them to allow air circulation. You can also use blowers and fans if your welding workshop lacks enough natural ventilation.

- **Enough lighting:** You need enough lighting in your workshop to ensure you can clearly see what you are welding. The lighting can be electric, natural, or a combination of both.

- **Large doors:** These are necessary if you intend to work on big welding projects; after all, you need large doors to get large things in and out of the workshop. A large roll-up or overhead door is most suitable.

- **Proper electrical service:** Ensure that your welding workshop or area is well serviced since welding machines and equipment in general use a lot of electricity.

- **Fire-resistant walls and floor**: You need to consider floors and walls that have properties that are resistant to fire. Have concrete floors without any carpeting. You can have cinder or plywood finishes for your workshop walls. Avoid wallpaper as the sparks can burn any loose wallpaper.

Sometimes, you may need to work on some welding projects from outside. Projects like an outdoor fireplace with bricks around it will need you to work on it outdoors because you have to position the firepit there.

In that case, you will need to;

- **Use a welding wall**: This can be in the form of a special welding screen or a solid sheet of metal, wood, or plastic. Have the wall close enough to your welding area. Using metal sheets can be dangerous, so watch out for magnetism, additional arc welding, and current shortcuts.

- **Check the weather**: You need to observe the weather conditions if you will weld from outside. Welding in stormy and windy weather can be difficult and dangerous. With electricity in use, standing in a puddle of water when welding can be dangerous as a wrong move can cause electric shock.
- **Get a welding tent or roof**: A welding tent is purposefully built for all-weather welding. It shields you from the harsh sun rays or rain.

How To Choose A Welding Table

For many of your welding projects, you need a strong, well-built, and reliable surface to use as a base. A normal wooden or metal table is not ideal for welding as it can burn from welding material spatter.

Choose a table made of a steel top and angle iron legs. For the table size, it depends on the size of your projects. Also, make sure that the height of the table is comfortable.

How To Choose Your Welding Machine

As illustrated earlier, welding machines come in different sizes, types, and prices. It all depends on the type of welding you plan on doing.

Here are a few things to consider when selecting a machine for your workshop.

- **Type and size of material**: As mentioned earlier, some machines can only weld a few different types of metals while others can weld a huge range of metals. If you are welding thin metals, most welding machines will do that. If you are welding thick metals, you may need to purchase a powerful enough machine. You will find more information on what machines can weld thin or thick materials in chapter 2.

- **Power source**: The power source here refers to the source of electrical energy such as power lines and batteries. The source of your electricity is also an important consideration when purchasing a welding machine. Make sure you purchase a machine that can work with your available power source.

- **Current**: Some welding machines use alternating current while others use direct current. Alternating current flows back and forth at regular intervals while direct current flows in one direction. When purchasing a welding machine, consider the type of electrical current you have available and prefer.

- **Availability of spare parts and service**: At one point, your welding machine will need service, no matter how good it is. Before purchasing one, find the nearest service point. You do not want to buy a machine that will require you to travel great distances to get servicing. Also, ensure that the spare parts for the machine you want to purchase are readily available. Buy from a professional retailer or manufacturer so that they can answer any questions you may have regarding these needs.

- **Welding process that suits you**: Welding machines are categorized depending on the welding process they perform. If your preferred welding method is MIG welding, then a MIG welding machine is what you need to purchase. The same goes for all welding machines.

In addition to the welding machine considerations, you can have a few accessories that can make your machine easier to use. They include;

- **Cable holder**: This is a hook mounted at the side of your machine that you can use to hold your ground cables.

- **Welding machine cart**: A welding cart is made of steel and has wheels that ease the work of moving your welding machine. You can weld one for yourself or purchase it from a welding store.
- **Storage drawer**: You can have small storage drawers for storing small machine parts when not in use.

Chapter 4: Welding Safety

One major thing about welding is that it utilizes materials and techniques that are hazardous. Currently, you will use huge amounts of electricity with most modern welding machines, which can be an electric shock risk.

You will also be working around extreme heat levels, which can damage your skin and property, not forgetting the sharp and heavy metals that can cause injuries.

Here are proper welding safety practices you need to be aware of and practice:

Always have the right fire extinguisher

With all the sparks flying around during welding, something may catch fire which is a real threat in a welding workshop. Therefore, it is advisable to have a fire extinguisher at all times in case of a fire.

Below are four types of fire extinguishers and what they do:

- **Class A**: This type of extinguisher takes care of fires that involve ordinary solid combustibles such as wood, cloth, or paper.

- **Class B**: This type of fire extinguisher takes care of fires that involve flammable liquids such as oils, paints, gasoline, grease, and alcohol.

- **Class C**: This type of fire extinguisher fights electrical fires. Note that you should not use water or foam-based fire extinguishers due to the risk of electric shocks.

- **Class D**: This type of fire extinguisher fights fires caused by flammable metallic substances such as magnesium, potassium, and sodium, which are extremely flammable.

When welding, you should have Class B and C fire extinguishers in cases of oil and electric fires. Sand is also useful in controlling metal fires, and it is helpful to keep a bucket of sand nearby if you do not have a special extinguisher.

However, staying safe is always the better option. You can minimize the use of fire extinguishers, but to do so, first, you must ensure the welding project you are working on does not have extra flammable material. For example, if the metal you are working with is oily or painted, ensure you clean it up before starting your project.

Wear the right clothing

You must keep your body from welding hazards, and to do so, you must wear protective clothing and the welding gear mentioned earlier. The metal sparks and slag flying around produced when welding can cause damage to your body if they get in contact with your skin.

Ensure that your clothes are free from flammable stuff such as paint and oil and that they are also close-fitting to prevent loose ends from catching fires. Clothing made of 100% cotton material is appropriate for welding. The fabric should also be thick to keep sparks from penetrating.

Here are examples of clothing details that you need to consider.

- **Shirts:** Wear long-sleeved shirts only. Do not fold your shirt sleeves; the purpose of the sleeves is to protect your hands from burns. Also, avoid shirts with front pockets, but if you wear one, ensure they have flaps covering them. Always tuck in your shirt.
- **Leather jacket:** The leather from your jacket protects you from flying sparks and slags when welding. You can substitute the jacket with leather sleeves if it gets too hot, but remember that this will leave your back unprotected.
- **Pants**: If you think you can weld in your shorts because it is summer and the heat is unbearable, then get rid of that thought. Those long pants that go all the way down covering your boots are just what you need. These will prevent the spark from contacting your legs, leaving you with burns. Forget the shorts as long as you are in your welding workshop!
- **Hats:** if you do not have a welding helmet, a welding hat will keep your hair from catching fire.
- **Boots:** As mentioned earlier, welding boots protect your feet from sparks and heavy metal injuries.
- **Gloves:** also mentioned in chapter 2.
- **Leather aprons:** A leather apron will protect your front body, especially the flying sparks.

Do not keep cigarettes or lighters in your pockets; they are a fire hazard should sparks get near.

Clean up your workspace

Before and after welding, ensure the welding area is clean and organized. By doing so, you get rid of any spilled flammable liquids that can cause fires in the workshop. Also, you prevent falling or tripping over tools and equipment on the way.

To maintain tidiness and cleanliness in your workshop;

- Set aside a place you can store all your welding tools and equipment. Ensure they all go to their correct place after completing a project. You can weld yourself a hanging shelf for all your welding tools, thereby saving space in your workshop.
- Clean all your welding tools and check for any damage after welding.
- Keep cables neat and disentangle them as messy tangles can cause tripping and falling.
- Store away any flammable items in your shop before you begin your welding project. However, when welding, handle with a lot of care those flammable gases you need to use, such as acetylene and natural gas. Have sealed containers for all flammable liquids and keep them in a flammable liquid's locker away from your welding workshop.

If you spill any flammable liquid, stop what you are doing and clean it up.

Adequate ventilation

Provide enough ventilation for your workshop to keep gases and fumes from the working area. You can use natural ventilation by opening doors and windows to let in the breeze. Another way you can allow ventilation in your workshop is by using the local exhaust ventilation method.

Local exhaust ventilation is a method engineered to protect workers from health risks caused by fumes. Breathing welding fumes and gases can cause health problems such as bronchitis, throat infection, lung cancer, and pneumoconiosis. The local exhaust ventilation control captures these hazardous fumes and gases and removes them from your workshop. Here is how an LEV system looks.

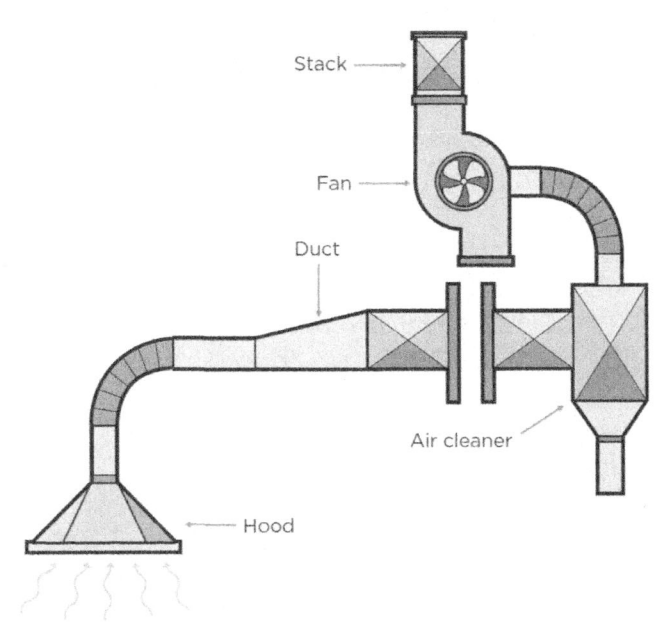

Chapter 5: Welding Tips for Beginners

Before starting any welding job, here are some tips to guide you.

Check the equipment

Before you begin that welding project, inspect the condition of the equipment you are using. Confirm things like proper connections of the gas tube, welding gun, and power cable. Ensure you are also using the right shielding gas and that the type and diameter of your filler material are correct.

Make sure that the feed rolls of the wire feeder are appropriate for the filler material and wire diameter you use. Next, detach your welding gun from the wire feeder and check if the type and size of the gun's liner are correct. Clean up the gas nozzle off any splashes from welding.

Check the welding torch speed

For successful welding, the correct speed of the welding torch is important. The speed affects the shape, heat input, and penetration of the weld. If the speed is too high, it may result in a very small weld penetration. On the other hand, the molten weld pool may be too much to manage if the speed is too slow.

To maintain the correct speed, weld approximately 10 cm and time it with a stopwatch to determine the speed in centimeters per minute.

Adjust the welding parameters

The speed motion of wire feed and welding current go hand in hand because when you increase or decrease the wire feed speed, the welding current follows. Ensure that the arc voltage is correct vis-à-vis the speed of the wire feed and welding current for proper welding.

To determine if the arc voltage is too low vis-à-vis the welding current and the wire feed speed, check if:

- There is a lot of spatters when welding.
- The arc produces a loud sound.

To determine if the arc voltage is high vis-à-vis the wire feed speed and welding current, check if:

- The arc produces a soft sound.
- The weld pool is wider.
- The arc is long.
- The volume of the filler material is large.

You can adjust the arc voltage to a workable figure by increasing or decreasing the wire feed speed. However, some welding machines automatically determine the correct arc voltage for the wire feed speed and welding current.

Use hot start and soft start features

The hot start is a manual metal arc welder feature that produces a large current when hitting the arc. This feature allows for easy fusing of metals at the beginning, allowing welding to continue smoothly. You can use the hot start feature when welding materials with good thermal conductivity, such as aluminum, since they generate faults easily at the beginning of welding —and the hot start can decrease them.

The soft start is a manual metal arc welder feature that gives off a low current when hitting the arc. When welding sheet metals such as steel, the soft start feature helps keep the edges of the sheets intact; you can adjust the power and duration of both features at the machine's control panel.

Other Welding Tips For Beginners

- **Prepare your materials for welding:** Before welding, clean your metal surface using a wire brush or sandpaper, then apply a coat of primer to protect it from corrosion.

- **Wear correct welding gear**: You need to protect your skin and clothes from the sparks and flame during the welding process. Therefore, you need to wear a welding helmet, boots, gloves, and sleeves. As earlier mentioned, each protective gear protects specific parts of your body.

- **Maintain a good working position:** The best position to do welding is downhand, which involves placing the working materials on a level to ensure you can do your welding in a natural position.

- **Use dry welding rods:** Avoid using damp rods since they cause the arc to be rough. Always store your welding rods in a sealed container when not in use.

- **Use the right type of tungsten.** Different types of metals work with different types of tungsten. For example, aluminum works well with green tungsten, while steel metals work well with red tungsten.

- **Be careful when working with stainless steel:** If you apply excessive heat to stainless steel, the material may become shapeless. Observe the color of the weld to know if you are applying the correct amount of heat. If the color of the weld is golden, then the heat applied is enough. If the weld color is dark to dirty gray, then the heat applied is excessive. To prevent this kind of problem, reduce the amps and increase the travel speed.

- **Do not melt the filler rod directly:** The weld will be weak if you melt your material directly.

- **Relax your hand**: Do not hold the gun too tightly. Relax your wrist to control the weld pool and have a good weld.
- **Have a welding mentor:** Training and practice make perfect, but having an experienced welder by your side enhances your learning process as you will get good advice that will get you to the next welding level.

Chapter 6: How to Know If You Are Welding Correctly

No matter what your welding project is, the quality of the finished weld is important. Here are some concrete ideas you can use to know if you are making your welds properly

The shielding gas residue and slag don't stick to your weld

You can tell that you have set your welding machine correctly when the waste materials such as weld slag and residue from the shielding gas do not stick to your welds.

When welding, you should use dry electrodes for them to be able to deposit quality welds. If the electrodes you are using are dry, the slag formed when the stick welding cools off and peels away easily from the weld instead of when the electrodes have moisture from the air. Also, the residue from the shielding gas should come off easily when you are MIG welding.

You have no holes on the welds

Porosity, which is having holes on welds, is a sign that your welds are weak, which also means that a problem probably occurred when welding. These holes can result from welding a dirty, wet, oily, or oxide-coated metal base. Also, not using enough shielding gas when TIG or MIG welding can cause holes. If you have no holes on your welds, you are probably doing it right!

Even distribution of welds between parts

When welding together two metal pieces, the molten pool that joins them should be distributed equally between the two pieces. You can make sure you do so by controlling the speed at which you make the welds.

Also, the type of filler metal you use and the thickness of the metals you are working with determine the size of your welds. However, even distribution of the welds is what matters.

There is no undercutting of the welds

You can be happy with the job you are doing if your welds do not contain undercutting, also referred to as underfill. Without a full joint, your welds become very weak. Excessive current when welding, using the wrong filler rods or electrodes, and holding your electrodes at the wrong angle are some of the main causes of weld undercuttings.

Full weld penetration

Penetration is the depth to which the molten metal goes from the surface of the base metal into the joint. For a strong weld, the penetration of the molten metal into the joint must be full because if it does not penetrate deep enough, the finished weld becomes weak and will eventually fail.

The weld is strong

The strength of the weld is an important consideration. You need to ensure your welds are strong enough to stand any forces applied to the joints. To ensure your welds are strong, use a filler rod or electrodes of a higher strength level than the base metal you are welding.

The weld has no overlap

A weld overlap occurs when the weld metal piles up in the joint. This results in the welds becoming very weak. Weld overlaps result from many factors, including holding the electrode improperly, low welding current, and excessive electrode speed travel. Checking these factors can help cut overlap problems.

Let us now get into the welding projects.

Chapter 7: Welding Projects

This chapter will give you detailed instructions for welding that you can try from the comfort of your welding workshop. There are several welding project ideas that you can build either for use at your home or to sell.

These are:

Outdoor Fireplace

Figure 1

Brick Surround

Stand Alone

Materials required:

- 3 Feet × 5.5 mild steel plate
- 4 inches × 12-inch mild steel plate
- 4 angle sections: 2 inch × 2 inches × 3/16 inch
- 105 feet mild steel rod: 25-inch diameter.

Tools required:

- Plasma cutter
- MIG, TIG, ARC, or GAS welder.
- Hacksaw or bandsaw
- Soapstone
- Angle grinder
- Grease remover

Steps:

1. Using a straight piece of metal and a plasma cutter, cut out the pattern you have marked for your outdoor fireplace.

2. On each steel sheet, mark lines on the areas you want to bend, and then using a cutting disc with a 4.5" angle grinder, cut along the line you marked for bending. Do not cut through. Bend each metal sheet toward the cut line to the angle you desire. Finally, fill the cut lines with a weld bead to restore the metal's strength.

3. Have the edges of the steel sheets ready for welding. Place them on your work surface and clean the areas you want to weld with a flap disc on an angle grinder.

4. Using welding magnets or clamps, position the metal sheets accurately, tack them together. Do the tacking from the bottom, then the top.

5. After tack-welding all four corners of the sheets, weld the top of each corner. Use an angle grinder to make them smooth.

Wine Bottle Holder

Materials required:

- 3.5 feet steel chain
- Spray paint and clear coat.
- An empty wine bottle.
- An empty 1000ml can.

Tools required

- MIG welder

Steps:

1. Place the steel chain around the 1000ml can in a uniform circle. Using a MIG welder, weld the chain links.
2. Arrange the rest of the chain perpendicularly to the welded circular chain base and weld the chain link. A strong welded base and top are necessary to bear the weight during bottle holding.

3. Using a diameter equal to a bottleneck, arrange part of the remaining chain in a circle and weld the links. Insert the wine bottle neck into the circle.
4. Weld the remaining hanging chain links.
5. Use an angle grinder or sandpaper to clean the slags and spatters from the welded chain and apply a coat of spray paint on it.

Barbecue Pit

Materials required:

- Mild steel angle iron 3/16 inches
- Square mild steel
- Ceramic insulation
- Expanded metal
- Angle iron
- Mild steel rod

Tools required:

- Angle grinder
- Tape measure
- Soapstone
- Drill
- Set square
- MIG welder

Steps:

1. Use square mild steel to cut two front legs [17-inches long]. Use angle iron to cut two back legs [each 20-inches long] and four side pieces [24-inches long].
2. On the back ends of the two side pieces, cut a 45-degree angle.
3. Weld two iron side pieces, one back leg and one front leg.
4. This welded frame acts as a guide for creating an identical side frame.
5. Cut 24-inches back piece using angle iron, then cut both ends of the back piece to a 45-degree angle. These should match the ends of the top side pieces you cut earlier.
6. Join the side frames to the back piece by welding them. Ensure that the frame is level, then use a level to align the upper side pieces.
7. Cut two 9-inches long pieces (each) using an angle grinder and weld them onto the back legs.
8. Use the square mild steel to cut two 24-inches long upper grill ends and two 30-inch-long lower grill ends. Cut 29 grill bars, 24-inch long each using the mild steel rod. Weld the grill bars to them.
9. Cut two 13-inch pieces of mild steel rod.
10. Bend each rod using a hammer to form upper grill handles. Ensure you bend the handles as close to being uniform as you can.
11. Weld the upper grill handles to the ends of the upper grill frame.

12. Finish up by applying boiled linseed oil to all parts except the handles and let dry for three days.

Welded Portraits Project

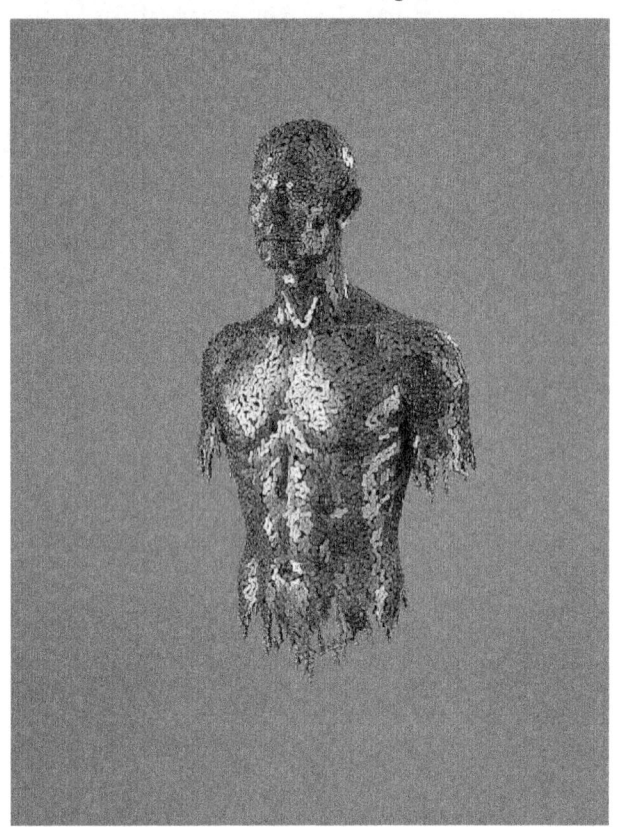

Materials required:

- 1/8 low carbon steel.
- Image of choice.
- Sandpaper.

Tools required:

- TIG welder

Steps:

1. Clean the metal well for welding preparation using sandpaper.
2. Trace the major lines of the image in oil pastel. Transfer the lines onto the metal. Ensure they are not too thick or thin to prevent distortion.
3. Use the TIG welder to weld the portrait. Use added filler metal to do the details. You can alter the bead length by increasing heat and adding more filler to fill in larger details such as hair, ears and nose.

Corner Desks

Materials required:

- Maple butcher block.
- 3 × 1.5 × 1/8 ″ tube steel.
- Rebar.
- 3/8 ″ bolts.
- Adjustable feet.
- Water lox tung oil finish.
- Degreaser.

Tools required:

- Circular saw
- Drill press
- Cutting bandsaw

- Angle grinder
- Hammer
- Welding magnets

Steps:

1. Hold the tabletop in place using clamps and cut it down to size using a circular saw. Then cut them down to 2 feet × 4 feet pieces.
2. Drill a semicircle into the desktop for the cord to pass through.
3. Connect the desktops with a corner bracket by screwing them in, then use a hammer to flatten them.
4. Apply the Waterlox tung oil for an amazing finish.
5. Cut the tube steel down to your desired size for the legs, and mark out the areas on top of the legs for drilling.
6. Use your welding magnet to position the four legs and weld them. Use the angle grinder to clean up all the welds.
7. Cut down the rebar to length, clean up the rust off of it with your grinder, then tack-weld it in place.
8. Measure out the areas you want the legs to sit and then mark the holes. Drill out holes for the threaded insert to fit in. After fitting in the threaded insert for the four legs, use a bolt with a couple of nuts for each leg. With the four legs in place, the corner table is now complete.

Firewood Storage Dolly

Materials required:

- 5 × 4-foot lengths of ¾ inch square tubing.
- 1 × 4-foot length of 1-inch square tubing
- 1 × 3-foot length 2″ × 2' hardwood
- 4 × 3.5-inch nails
- 2 × inch nails

Tools required:

- Chop saw
- Angle grinder

- Welder
- Clamps
- Disc sander

Steps:

1. Cut 4 pieces of 1" feet square tubing to 2" × 18" and 2" × 8" long magnets or clamps to position the pieces and clean them up using an angle grinder with the flap disc.

2. Cut steel 24 inches long, which when bent is 14 inches l0ng. Use your disc sander to round the edges. Remove the sharp edges using your scroll bender for a neater finish.

3. Put everything together once you finish bending all the four scrolls.

4. Clamp up the rack's legs and tack weld them in. Add some more welds to strengthen the frame.

5. Use your square plugs to seal the holes at the end of the frame. To prevent corrosion and add a touch to the rack, apply a metal paint coating.

Hanging Shelves

Materials required:

- 2" × 10" pine board
- ½" paddle bit.
- Drill press
- Sandpaper
- Cloth {2 or 3}
- Stain or paint

Tools required:

- Drill press
- Sandpaper

- Circular saw
- Soapstone
- Level
- Drill
- MIG welder

Steps:

1. Mark the area of the wall where you want your shelf. Use a 1/2 inches driller to drill holes for the shelf anchors.
2. Take your toggle bolts and insert them into the holes you drilled. Tighten them against the wall.
3. Gather all your materials together and cut all the steel parts. Use an angle grinder to remove the waste.
4. Weld the brackets. Start by laying your cut metal tubing at right angles. Use welding metals or clamps to hold them in position. Weld them, then drill holes depending on the size of screws you use for mounting.
5. Prepare the shelves. Cut rebar 78 inches long for 7 inches long overlap on either side of the brackets. Beat them with a rotating motion using a hammer and a short-chain length, then use a brush to put a paint coating.
6. Paint the brackets.
7. Mount the brackets and shelves. Start by positioning the brackets to the anchoring points on the wall and then use the screwdriver to insert the screws in each bracket.
8. Once the brackets are in place, put all four shelves on loosely first. Mark 1 inch and 6 inches from the end, measure ½ inches from the line, then drill a hole into the shelves that go through the metal. Insert the screws.

Steel Flower Welding Project

Materials required:

- 64 spoon handles cut 2 ½ inches long.
- 4 spoon handles cut 3 ¼ inches for the leaves.
- 1 gear for the base.
- 2 circles, 1½ inches by 3/8 inches thick.
- 1 circle, 2 by ¼ inches thick.
- 2 inner valve springs.
- 2 round bars, ¼ inches for the stems – one 12 inches long and the other 9 inches long.

Tools required

- TIG welder

Steps:

1. Arrange 16 spoon handles such that they face down around one of the 1½ inches circles, ensuring you space them evenly around the circle.
2. Tack all petals in place and weld them all. The spoons act as the petals.
3. Arrange a second set of 16 spoons, tack all petals and weld them. Again, the spoons act as the petals.
4. Repeat these steps for the other flowers.
5. Bend the stems to look natural, then weld them to the back of the flowers.
6. Attach the flower to its base by welding the taller flower at a slight angle slightly off the center.
7. Attach the shorter flower to the gear base off the side by welding it.
8. Bend the spoon handles that have remained (they should be of 3 ¼ inches long) to look like leaves. Weld them to the stems.

Height Adjusting Stools

Materials required:

- 4 × 22″ lengths of mild steel square tube
- 3 × 12″ lengths of mild steel square tube
- 4 × 14″ 45-degree mitered lengths of mild steel square tube
- 4 × 8.5″ 45-degree lengths of flat bar steel
- 2 × 12″ × 12″ birch plywood squares
- Coupler nut

Tools required:

- TIG welder
- Angle grinder
- Soapstone
- Bandsaw
- Drill

Steps:

1. Cut 4 triangle pieces of plywood about 2 inches that fit the length of the coupler nut.
2. Mark the middle where you will attach the coupler nut.
3. Use welding magnets to keep the coupler nut in place, tack-weld the coupler nut into place, then add the triangle gussets, ensuring it is square to the metal plate.
4. Weld along all sides of the triangles. Weld a nut inside a pipe for the base of the stool.
5. Cut the tube steel at a 45-degree angle for the base of the stool. Use magnets and clamps to position the lower parts of the stool vertically.
6. Tack-weld the legs to the base of the stool, then weld them until they are stable.
7. Finally, attach the seat to the legs by drilling holes and inserting screws through the metal and seat.

Star Decor

Materials required:

- 4mm steel rod
- LED warm white tree lights
- Cable ties
- Spray paint

Tools required:

- MIG welder

Steps:

1. Get your bits together, then cut the rod to length. For the external star, cut 10 pieces of 7 inches each; for the short internal star, cut 10 pieces of 3 inches each, and for the long internal star, cut 10 pieces of 9 inches each.

2. Clean up the ends using an angle grinder for welding. Weld three cut-off nails to act as a jig for welding the five

arms of the star.

3. Mark the welding areas. Position the first pieces of the outer star on the jig and weld the ends of the five arms on both sides.

4. Weld the inner joints of the star arms. Position the short rods from the inner joints to meet at a point and weld the point together.

5. Weld the star point ends of the long inner rods to the inner middle point. Flip over and weld the other side. Use your angle grinder to clean the weldments to a nice finish.

Welding Trolley Project

Materials required

- Square tubing
- Angle iron
- Steel tubing
- Heavy-duty casters
- A small scrap of flat bar

Tools required:

- MIG welder
- Welding magnet
- Cut off wheels

- Speed square
- Metal bandsaw

Steps:

1. Gather the square tubing, angle iron, and steel tubing.
2. Draw 45-degrees angles on both ends of the square tubing using a speed square. Cut the angles marked using a bandsaw. Use the piece as a template to cut a similar piece.
3. Mark and cut two shorter pieces for the top frame.
4. Hold the pieces in place using a welding magnet, square the joints using a speed square, then tack-weld each joint before welding them.
5. Fully weld the joints using the MIG welder. Use the angle grinder to smoothen the welds.
6. Repeat the process on the larger bottom frame.
7. Cut four large pieces of angle iron to use as the poles. Hold them in place [perpendicular to the top frame and bottom frame] using a speed square and tack weld them.
8. Fully weld all joints for both frames. Use the angle grinder to clean up the welds.
9. Turn the frame upside down and mark the width of the area between the bottom frame. Using the measurements, cut two pieces of square tubing and weld them in place. These two pieces act as cross supports.
10. Using the bandsaw, cut down pieces of the steel tubing for the top work surface. Line the pieces with the side of the frame and tack them in place until you reach the end.
11. Weld the heavy-duty caster wheels into each bottom frame corner.

12. Mark out the size of the bottom shelf on an expanded steel sheet and use a cut-off wheel to cut it to size. Notch out excess steel with a grinding disc to ensure it sits on the sides properly. Cut down a smaller piece of the steel sheet for the top shelf.

13. Tack both shelves around the edges.

14. Cut the handle pieces as desired, tack them on each side and then fully weld them together.

15. Use the bandsaw to notch the small scrap of flat bar that acts as a peg for the chain. Weld the piece into place.

16. Load up the pieces on the cart, and that's it!

Hanging Steel Pan Rack

Materials required:

- 1.25″ square tubing, 3/32″ wall thickness
- 14 × ¼-20 threaded steel hooks
- 2 × 1.25″ × 1.25″ flat plate steel [1/8″ thickness]
- 24 × 1.25″ OD steel washers
- 4 × ¼-20 thread drywall anchors
- 24 × ¼-20 nuts
- Short length of chain

Tools required:

- MIG welder

- Angle grinder
- Cut off wheel
- Grinding wheel
- Steel chop saw
- Hand drill
- 90-degree square

Steps:

1. Using your chop saw, cut square tubing 1 × 48" long and 2 × 8" long. Place both ends of the 48 inches tubing with one end of each 8 inches tubing together. Cap the open ends of the short pieces with thick, cut square pieces of steel. Weld them into place.

2. Use your angle grinder to clean up the joints. Use the 90-degree square to arrange the pieces at right angles and tack-weld them together. Adjust where necessary, then fully weld the joints.

3. Smoothen the welds using your angle grinder for a professional look.

4. Use a 1/4" drill bit to drill the holes for the kitchenware. Drill through both tube walls and space them 10" apart to give enough room for each pan.

5. Drill a hole into all four corners of the rack, then install the nuts, hooks, and washers. Install the hooks in the four corners pointing up while the other hooks point down. Install a nut and washer on each side of the hooks. You should arrange them in the following order: nut-washer-hook-washer-nut-hook, and tighten the nuts to secure the hooks in place.

6. Cut the chain into four. The link segment depends on your ceiling height —Mark out four points on your ceiling in a 50″ × 10″ rectangular pattern. Use your drill to drill a hole large enough to fit your drywall anchors at each marked point. Install the hooks with a washer and a nut.

7. Hang up the rack with the chain links and start using it — no more filling up your drawers with pans!

Simple Pencil Holder

Materials required:

- 10.5″ of square steel tubing with inner dimensions of 3/8″ × 3/8″.
- 12-gauge steel sheet

Tools required:

- Files
- Spray paint
- Hacksaw
- MIG Welder

Steps:

1. Cut the steel tubing into four sections at 3 inches, 2.75 inches, 2.5 inches, and 2.25 inches long, respectively. Use

your angle grinder to smoothen the top and bottom of each piece. Try to stand them with the bottom parts down. If they do not stand straight, use your file to file them until they can stand without wobbling.

2. Use the gauge sheet to cut 2 inches by 4 inches rectangle to act as the base. Use the angle grinder or file to have smooth edges.

3. Place the tubing pieces you cut earlier on the center of the base and use your clamps or welding magnet to hold them in place.

4. Weld them to the base using your MIG welder. Clean up the welds with the wire brush and file. You can leave it there or use spray paint to add a more stylish look.

Welding Table

Materials Required

- 4 square mild steel pieces 31.5 inches long
- 1 square mild steel piece 43 inches long
- 4 square mild steel pieces 48 inches long
- 4 square mild steel pieces 30 inches long
- 1 square mild steel piece 25 inches long
- 8 flat bar pieces 30 inches long
- 4 2-inch caster wheels with breaks

Tools Required

- Drop saw
- Angle grinder
- Welder
- Set square

- Paint and brushes
- Spirit levels

Steps

1. Using the drop saw, cut the 31 inches square metal bars into 45-degrees cuts on both sides. Cut all the 48 inches and 30 inches long metal bars into the same 45-degrees cuts, making a total of 8 bars cut on both sides.
2. Cut all the remaining metal bars into straight cuts.
3. Align the square metal bars you cut earlier into two sets of rectangles. Using the set square, make sure the corners are a 90-degrees, then weld them together and fill the gaps.
4. Add the 25-inch square metal bar on one rectangle set in a vertical position. The rectangle forms the bottom part of the welding table. Use a spirit level to ensure the surface is flat before welding.
5. Place a cut 31-inch square metal bar on each corner of the frame. Place a second frame atop the vertical metal bars and fully weld them together.
6. Turn the structure upside down and place the caster wheels on each bottom corner. Fully weld them in place.
7. In the middle of the top rectangle, place the 48 inches square metal bar horizontally and level with the top frame. Position it using your welding magnets and weld it in place.
8. Place all the 5-inch flat metal bars across the top frame, with a spacing of 2 inches in between each bar. Position them with the clamps or welding magnets. Tack weld the middle part and sides of the flat bars.

9. Fully weld the flat metal bars to the top frame. Use your angle grinder to clean up the welds and smoothen the edges.

10. You can finish up the table by adding a coat of paint as desired.

Campfire Grill

This grill is portable and adjustable to suit your height.

Materials required:

- 3 pieces of square tubing 22 inches long
- 2 pieces round stock 10 inches long
- 2 pieces of square tubing 2 inches long
- 2 pieces of square tubing 4 inches long
- 1 piece of square tubing 10 inches long
- One rectangular steel grill grate 14-inch × 22-inches
- 1 piece of angle iron 74 inches long

Tools Required

- Angle grinder
- Hacksaw or bandsaw
- File

- Soapstone
- Tape measure
- MIG or stick welding machine
- Grease remover

Steps:

1. Using your soapstone and tape measure, measure and mark all the areas as desired. Cut the three 22-inch steel tubing. Use the file to straighten the edges.
2. Cut the angle iron into four pieces to form a 14-inch × 22-inch rectangular frame. Cut the round stock so you have 24 14-inches pieces, then smoothen all rough edges of the pieces with a file.
3. Place the three 22-inch pieces of steel tubing on your welding table with two of the pieces on top of the third piece to form a u-shape. Tack weld the joints together.
4. Turn over the frame and fully weld the joints from the bottom.
5. Turn the frame back over and weld the joints from the top.
6. Place your angle iron pieces for the grill grate on the frame to form a 22-inch × 14-inch rectangle. Ensure the corners are at a 90-degrees angle using a set square, then tack weld them together.
7. Lay the 24 pieces of round stock inside your angle iron frame, space them as desired, then tack weld them in place. Fully weld them on the grill grate.
8. Place one 2-inch tubing piece between the bottom piece of the u-shaped frame, tack it into a 10-degrees angle

and fully weld it in place.

9. Bend the two 10-inches pieces of round stock to form a u-shape. They keep the base of the grill firm to prevent it from moving when you move the grill grate on and off the fire.

10. Tack the other 2-inch steel tubing onto the long side of the grill grate frame. Center it halfway down the 22-inch tubing, then weld it in place.

11. Finish the grill by adding a coating of grill paint.

Suspension Stool

Materials required:

- Circular steel
- Spring
- Gauge tubing 21 inches long
- Gauge tubing 12 inches long
- 2″ 3/8 tubing 1/4″ gauge

Tools Required

- Cut off wheel
- Flapper disc
- Angle grinder
- Welder

- Wire wheel
- Set square
- Measuring tape
- Wire brush
- Hammer
- Level

Steps

1. Use your angle grinder to clean up the edges of the circular steel, bevel the edges of the gauge tubing, and bring it down to bare steel.
2. Use your set square to stand the 2 ″ 3/8 tubing straight at a 90-degrees angle. Use your welding magnets to keep it in place, then tack weld all the way around and fully weld it.
3. Use your angle grinder to grind the base to bare steel, then grind it with a flapper disc to make it shine.
4. Place the tubing on the seat, level it straight using your welding magnet, then tack-weld all around it. Fully weld it to the base.
5. Slide the spring over the tubing attached to the seat.
6. Slide the tubing attached to the seat into the tubing attached to the base and flip it upright.
7. Give the stool a finish with a clear coating of paint.

Simple Garden bench

Materials Required

- Steel 30mm × 6mm
- 3 pieces of 75mm × 50mm wood
- 2 pieces of wood 50 inches long

Tools Required

- Angle grinder
- Welder
- Screws
- Drill
- Clamps
- Tin can
- Jigsaw
- Carriage bolts

Steps

1. Create the template to have the size of the bench and the form for bending the steel.
2. Cut steel into two, 2.1 m each. Cut the wood into three pieces, 75mm × 50mm each.
3. Take the wood pieces and use the tin to create the curved part of the bench. Mark a curve on the wood using the tin can and cut it using a jigsaw.
4. Fix the first piece of the curved wood to the template with screws and then clamp one of the pieces of steel to it. Bend the steel around the curved part of the wood.
5. After bending the first part, attach the second piece of wood with screws and clamps, then bend the steel back around it. Attach the third piece and bend the steel the same way.
6. Bend the steel to about a 7-degrees angle using your set square to form the backrest.
7. Cut off the excess steel at the front using an angle grinder, then use this to create the seating part of the bench. Weld the pieces together.
8. Cut the brackets for the bolts from the scrap pieces of steel using the angle grinder. Weld the brackets to the seating part and backrest of the bench.
9. Use a grinding disc to clean up all the welds and then use a drill to drill holes through the steel for inserting the bolts when attaching the backrest and seat.
10. Have the wood for the seat and backrest 50 inches long, and drill holes through them for the bolts.

Use carriage bolts 50mm long. Insert the bolts through the steel and wood, then secure with a spanner.

Modern Outdoor Table

Materials required

- 3/4 inches steel bar
- 3/4 inches steel angle iron
- 2 ½ steel flat bar
- Paint
- Primer

Tools required

- Welder
- Angle grinder
- Metal cut off saw

Steps

1. Have a sketch for the legs, then trace it out on the ¾ inches steel bar with a silver pen. Use a cold saw to cut out each piece from the marked lines.
2. Use the angle grinder to bevel the edges of the legs where you will join them. Use clamps to position the pieces, tack-weld them together, then fully weld each joint.
3. Use the angle grinder to smoothen the welds.
4. Cut two ½ inches bar and weld with a full bead to the top of each leg to attach the table—drill holes along the bar for inserting the screws which will attach the board to the bar.
5. For more stability, connect the legs with long stretchers. Cut two bars, tack weld them together with long stretches, and fully weld them in place.
6. Cut down the wood into two pieces ½ inches wide each.
7. Use an angle iron frame to wrap the top of the table.
8. Cut the miters on the metal using a cold saw and weld them on corners. Add cut flat bars in the middle of the boards to hold them in place.
9. Place the wood pieces for the table on the bars, then apply oil to all the boards and a few coats of paint. Use primer for the base.
10. Predrill all pieces of wood, then lay out one board at a time and screw it to the center of the flat bar. Leave a small gap for water drainage. Finally, attach the tabletop to the legs through the drilled holes using screws.

NOTE: For grills, barbecue pits, and outdoor fireplaces, ensure you use paint that can withstand high temperatures because you will expose them to high levels of heat. Also, do not paint any surface of your grill or barbecue pit on which you will cook food.

TIG-Welded Fruit Bowl

Materials required

- 16 inches gauge stainless steel.
- Stainless steel TIG filler rod 1/3 inches
- Clear metal wax

Tools required:

- TIG welder
- Tungsten grinder
- Angle grinder
- Sandpaper
- Pen and paper or sketching software

Steps

1. Design the piece using the sketching software or pen and paper. Create a faceted bowl but keep it simple.
2. Trace the design on the stainless steel. Using a plasma cutter, cut out the pieces. The measurements are as

desired. Use an angle grinder to smoothen the edges.

3. Set up the TIG welder. Start by tack welding all of the pieces together, making sure the edges are lined up properly.

4. Use clamps to position the pieces in place and fully weld all the corners and edges.

5. Using your angle grinder, smoothen the outside surface to create a seamless and shiny finish.

6. You can apply clear wax on it for the finish.

Metal Storage Rack

Materials Required

- 10-gauge steel sheet
- 6.35cm steel box section

Tools Required

- Angle grinder
- Mig welder
- Drill
- Drill bits
- Bench shear
- Circular saw

Steps

1. Measure up the width, depth, and height you desire for your rack.
2. Cut two lengths at the height measurement.
3. Cut three lengths at width measurement and twelve lengths at depth.
4. Take the gauge steel sheet and cut 14 square pieces at 90mm × 90mm. Drill a hole in each corner of the square pieces.
5. Lay out the height and lengths of the box flat on your work surface. Place one length at 500mm from the top, one at 1250mm from the top, and the other across the top of the upright height lengths.
6. Fully weld each of the pieces together.
7. Take two of your squares and weld them to the bottom of two upright heights.
8. Take the remaining 12 square pieces and the rest of the depth pieces and weld one square on one end of each depth length.
9. Take your depth pieces and weld them at the same time along your length sections of the box.

Chapter 8: Welding Repair

This chapter guides you on using your welding techniques to repair metal items, whether it is your tools, part of your equipment, a piece on some machinery, or other metal objects.

What Is Repair Welding?

Repair welding is a technique used to remove material that is damaged, either by arc gouging, plasma cutting, or oxyfuel, then the element is welded and used as a joint for the material on either side of the crack.

For successful welding repair, here are a few things to consider:

- **The type of metal used**: Certain metals work well with specific types of welding techniques. For example, TIG welding is great for repairing aluminum, stick welding is good for repairing iron, and MIG welding works well with steel.

- **The welding equipment you have**: Consider what welding equipment you have first before deciding to repair anything. For example, if you have a TIG welding machine only, you probably need to focus on welds you can make using the TIG machine.

- **Condition of the base metal**: If the metal is just in bad shape, you only need stick welding.

- **Welding process**: If you are using the MIG welding process, you must plan for repairs you can weld using the MIG process. The same applies to all other welding processes.

- **The cause of the damage**: Identify the causes of, for example, cracks on the piece you want to repair if possible. That way, you can lessen some of their negative effects.

- **If the old product had a complicated design:** The original piece may have had a complex design. Therefore, you may need to simplify it with your repair weld.

Getting Started On Weld Repairs

After considering all the above tips, you can now get ready to repair your welds. Here's how:

Prepare your workspace

By now, you are familiar with welding safety tips. Well, the same goes for your welding repair' workspace preparation. You must observe all welding safety measures as earlier discussed.

Prepare the piece you are to repair

Carefully clean up the metals you will be repairing. Most of the items need a thorough cleaning from oil, grease, and paint, especially if they have been in use for quite a while. Besides, clean metals can improve the quality of your repair welds.

Gather your tools and equipment

Here are the tools and equipment you should have close at hand.

- **Welding machine**: This is the most important one; no welding can take place without a welding machine.
- **Angle grinder**: When making repairs, you are most likely to use an angle grinder a lot for cleaning up metal and smoothening welds and sharp edges.
- **Welding materials**: These include filler rods, filler metals, shielding gas, and electrodes. Choose materials that suit the repair job.

- **Soapstone and tape measure**: Measuring and marking the damaged areas on metal for repair is one of the things you must do for accuracy.

- **Paint and paintbrushes**: To prevent the piece you have repaired from corrosion and rust, and also for a professional finish, you may want to give it a coat or two of paint.

- **Lighting**: Proper lighting is very important as it is important to see well when you are welding to repair a broken piece of metal.

Consider the cracks

Weld cracks are the most serious types of welding defects. Cracks reduce the strength of a material, so you have to repair them immediately after they occur if you want your metals to work as they should.

The following are different crack types you need to understand before performing welding repairs.

- **Cold cracks** occur when the metal temperature has gone down after welding. It can take hours or even days for the cold cracks to form on the welded metal. Steel is the most affected by these cracks.

- **Hot cracks** form during welding when the temperatures are as high or above 10,000 degrees centigrade.

- **Crater cracks** may occur at the end of the welding process when the welding pool does not have enough volume so as to overcome the weld metal's shrinkage.

Cracks occur when welding in the following ways:

- Rapid heating or cooling of the base metal.

- Contaminants in the filler metal or the metal.
- Contaminants in the electrodes.
- Higher carbon content in the base metal than in the filler material.
- Contact of thick metal plates before welding, causing too much stress on the weld, resulting in cracking.
- Thick metal plate.

Here's how you can overcome them:

- Preheat the metal as required.
- Remove impurities.
- Provide proper cooling of the weld area.
- Use the right type of metal.
- Use the correct welding speed.
- Use the correct joint design.
- Fill the cracks effectively to prevent any crater cracks.

Protect adjacent machinery

When repairing welding machinery, protect the parts still intact from welding spatter, sparks, and any other hazardous material generated from the welding repair process.

Disassembly

For machinery repairs, disassemble the machinery from the machinery frames —this may not apply to simple repair jobs.

Bracing and clamping

You may need to apply bracing and clamping if the repair job is complex due to the heaviness of machine or equipment parts. You can temporarily weld braces to the structure you are repairing.

Grind and clean

This is an important stage of repair welding as the resulting welds may not be as desired. Grind the welds to smoothen and clean before and after repair.

Post-Repair Operation

Now that you completed the repair, you probably will not leave it at that.

Here are a few steps to follow to ensure a quality job.

- **Inspection**: Inspect the finished weld for smoothness and quality since it replaces the original metal of high quality.
- **Cleaning up**: Use your angle grinder to smoothen the welds and clean weld spatters, slags, and grinding dust.
- **Repainting**: After cleaning up the repair area, you should repaint it and re-grease other parts in preparation for the machine re-operation.
- **Re-assembly**: After painting and cleaning, you must return the parts of machinery you de-assembled.

Printed in Great Britain
by Amazon